DEPARTMENT OI

TRAINING AND INSTRUCTION

PHYSICAL TRAINING CENTER

AT

JOINVILLE-LE-PONT

MANUAL

FOR

HAND TO HAND COMBAT

December 1st, 1917

TRANSLATOR'S PREFACE

———

    This manual is truly what I would call a hidden gem of combatives. The year is 1917 and France has already been slugging it out in the trenches with *Les Boches* for nearly three years. The war that both sides in their overweening chauvinism had foreseen as an easy win had turned into a murderous stalemate with the *Poilus* hammering away at *Fritz* for a gain of 300 meters that would be taken from them a day or two later. No man's land was a nightmare of craters, barbed wire, and unexploded shells littered horribly with bodies and parts of bodies in every conceivable stage of decomposition. Glorious patriotic visions had given way to the brutal reality of the new modern warfare, and it finally became clear to the French command that any guide to combat that was not entirely based in reality would only harm their troops. With this in mind a supplementary training manual was devised to "set forth only some of the **most effective techniques**". This means that whatever instruction had been given in the past, before the ugly realities of the trenches became clear, it was not enough to prepare a recruit for what he would actually be facing. This manual served to fill the knowledge gap.

All of those who take an interest in that side-category of the martial arts known as *combatives* understand the power of a threat response that is *crude but effective.* When someone is proactively trying to kill you, you may well forget your own name, much less a long sequence of movements you studied once a week some time ago. Those who, like myself, are fans of the William E. Fairbairns school of not getting killed will be pleased with this little work. Those with a taste for history will be educated and amused by the fine old photos of a genuine 1917 *Poilu* strangling, gouging, and bayoneting an authentically dressed German *Dreckfresser.* And who knows? Maybe someday one of these *"coups"* will save your skin on the battlefield of life.

--*Matthew Lynch, 2018*

TABLE OF CONTENTS

Chapter 1

1. Take him down and put him out of the fight

2. Take him down, arm hold.

3. Face smash

4. Punch

5. Wrist bone strike

6. Front kick

7. Chassé kick

8. Strangulation

9. Strangulation from behind

KNIFE ATTACK

Chapter 2

Defend & Counterattack

1. When the enemy attacks you with:

   A punch

   A kick

   A grab

   A choke

The enemy attacks from behind

Chapter 3

Defend & Counterattack

1. For a knife attack
2. A high knife attack
3. A low knife attack
4. A bayonet attack

Chapter 4

Taking a prisoner.

HAND TO HAND COMBAT:

General observations

The goal of this pamphlet is to complete the instruction regimen for bayonet and hand-to-hand combat as it is administered at C. I. P. [Center for Physical Instruction] de Joinville and to set forth only some of **the most effective** techniques among those demonstrated in the exercises on attack and defense.

The knowledge of these techniques, which are simple and straightforward, will reinforce the idea that although a soldier be **disarmed**, if he is **animated by the spirit of remaining on the offense**, he has nothing to fear from any enemy, whoever it may be.

The 1st chapter deals with putting the enemy **out of combat definitively**, and the different attacks that a soldier without a weapon can carry out, be it to **kill** his enemy or **simply put him out of the fight**.

To this we have added the most deadly cuts that can be given with the trench knife.

Chapters 2 and 3 deal with **defense and above all counter-attacks** for the unarmed soldier against both an armed and a disarmed adversary, attacking him be it with a knife or a rifle with a bayonet. Defense has no value **save when it is followed immediately by a counter** which will put the enemy out of the fight, be it for good or only for a time.

Chapter 4 deals with the best way for a soldier without a weapon or assistance to take a prisoner who is ready to fight or to flee.

METHOD OF INSTRUCTION

Instruction consists in frequently repeating all of the strikes and holds to the right and the left (without actually dealing the blows or administering the holds fully during study) so that the soldier arrives, by instinct, at being able to choose the best procedure according to the circumstances of combat.

The instructors must watch over those procedures for putting an enemy out of the fight definitively, which will end each exercise, to see that the students are going through the motions.

CHAPTER 1

ATTACK

You are unarmed and you are facing an enemy who is also unarmed. Do not allow him to initiate any attempt at a strike, but throw yourself on him and bring him down with a trip. Your adversary has his left leg forward. Grab his left arm with your right hand, gripping his uniform above the elbow. With your left hand grab his left shoulder or his combat webbing on that side. At the same time pivot to the right on your right leg and place your left leg against his left leg, your toes in the dirt and your heel elevated behind his heel, your calf up against his calf (above) without engaging the rest of the leg overmuch.

Fig. 1

With your left leg tensed, pull his leg from under him vigorously. With your right hand pull him toward you while with your left hand you push down and to the right.

Continue the movement so as to throw the enemy on his stomach while keeping him up against you (fig. 2, below).

Fig. 2

Pass your forearm under his chin and quickly straddle his back with your knee on his spine and your other leg splayed out for balance. Pull his head back violently so as to fracture the cervical vertebrae. If the enemy has his right leg forward, perform the same takedown to your left, reversing the rest of the attack in turn.

Fig. 3

You also have the non-lethal option (taking a prisoner). Once you have taken your enemy down with the preceding method, grab his wrist with both hands.

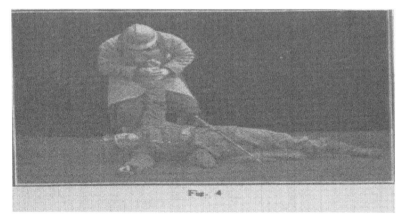

Fig. 4

Pull the arm up so that the forearm is between your thighs. Your knees are slightly flexed. Drop your right knee on his neck and your left knee on his side. With your left hand, pull his left arm back and to the left with his elbow resting on your left thigh and the back of his hand facing the ground. With your right hand grab his forehead and pull his skull backwards while squeezing with your knees and your left hand. Yank his right arm down fiercely with the aid of your body weight while your left thigh squeezes in the opposite direction.

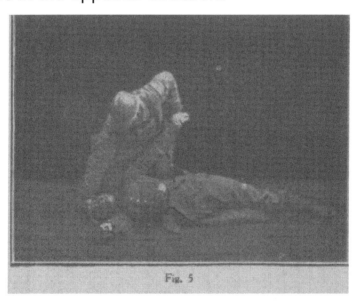
Fig. 5

This same procedure can be brought to bear on the other arm.

Before making an attack it is best, according to circumstances, to blind the enemy with the following procedure: Spread your fingers and fling your hand into his face. Your fingers go to his eyes, your palm to his chin and nose, and your thumb is under his chin.

Fig. 6

With one hand feign a blow to the opponent's face while your other hand strikes the side of his jaw or the bottom of it. Your fist is closed and delivered *with the weight of your whole body behind it.* Take advantage of your enemy's surprise to take him down and put him out of the fight for good. This strike can be delivered without a feint preceding it.

With one hand feign a strike to the enemy's face while the other administers a sharp blow to his neck at three fingers'

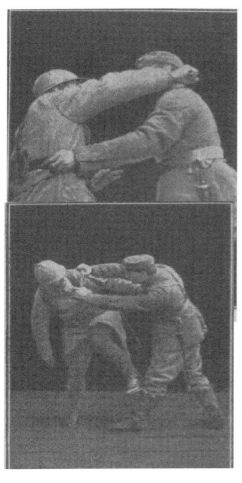

width behind his ear with the *with the inside edge of the wrist beneath the thumb (fig. 7, left).*

Take advantage of the stunning effect to take him down and put him out of the fight for good.

Fling the toe of your boot into his genitals.

Turn to the side and lift then lightly flex your leg before smashing the outside heel of your boot-sole into the enemy's knee, tibia, or foot. Take advantage of the stunning effect of the kick to unbalance your enemy and put him out of the fight for good. Grab the enemy with both hands, your arms somewhat bent, your fingers clutching his neck and your thumbs on either side of his adam's apple. Squeeze in

Fig. 9

with your thumbs and try to make them touch. At the same time put your left leg against his left leg, with your left buttock against his left thigh, and continue to strangle him or take him down to put him out of the fight for good (fig. 9).

To take him down to your left, reverse the instructions taking left for right.

This manner of attack can follow a strike or a kick.

Fig. 10

If your enemy has his back to you:

Jump on him and quickly encircle his neck with your left arm, placing the inside edge of your forearm up against his adam's apple. Grab your left wrist with your right hand and squeeze then enemy's neck between your forearm and shoulder. You can reset your grip by kicking the back of his calf muscles when needed (fig. 10, above). Bring him down and lean over him with your upper body [on the back of his head] until he is strangled or his neck is broken (fig. 11, below).

This hold can be performed with either arm.

Fig. 11

NOTE:

ATTACK WITH A KNIFE

With your free hand throw a strike at the enemy's face while with your knife you strike at his lower abdomen, his side, his groin, or the lower sides of his neck (carotids).

CHAPTER II:

DEFENSE & COUNTER

The unarmed adversary.

I. When an enemy facing you attacks:

1. With a punch

Avoid his strike either by intercepting it with your bent arm (then respond using this same arm for a punch or a wrist-bone strike), then jump on your enemy and strangle him or take him down to put him definitively out of the fight.

2. With a kick

Avoid his kick by moving to the side or jumping away from the attacking limb, then jump on the enemy and give him a punch or a wrist-bone strike, or strangle him. Better still you should take him down to put him out of the fight for good.

3. With a body grab

If the enemy grabs you, make him let go either by a knee to his genitals, or a slam to his face with your thumb under his chin, your fingers digging into his face while you push his head back (fig. 12). Take him down and put him out of the fight for good.

4. By strangulation

Fig. 12

Grab his left wrist with both hands and pivot rapidly to your left to place your right buttock against his left side (fig.13) while pulling his outstretched arm best you can under your right armpit with the palm of his hand facing up. Bend your upper body to the right while squeezing the enemy's arm beneath yours, and quickly lift your hands skyward (fig. 14). Now throw him to the ground and put him out of the fight for good.

Fig. 13

This hold can be applied to either arm.

Fig. 14

II. When the enemy attacks from behind:

He is holding you with his hands clasped over your chest, your stomach, or your neck.

To make him let go grab his arms and give him a heel-stomp (to his knee, tibia, or toes), then turn and take him down and put him out of the fight for good, or grab a thumb or finger with your inverted hand with your thumb against his hand (fig. 15). Pull back violently with your hand pivoting around your thumb, turning around fully without letting go, then unbalance the enemy and put him out of the fight for good.

Fig. 15

CHAPTER III

DEFENSE &

COUNTER

The armed adversary

I. Counter knife attack

Your enemy tries to stab you in your upper body (neck, chest). Block the stab with your left forearm striking his right wrist while leaping forward and to the left (fig. 16, left) bringing your right leg behind his right leg. At the same time pass your right arm over his right arm. With your right hand above his right elbow, grab his left hand and bring your left elbow to the right, pulling your hands down strongly and somewhat to your left (fig. 17, below) while inclining your upper body forward and throwing the foe to the ground. Seize the knife and and stab him. If the adversary holds the knife in his left hand, block it with your right forearm and execute the hold by reversing the instructions already given.

2. Counter the low line knife attack.

If the enemy wants to stab you in your lower torso (stomach, groin) block the cut with your left wrist against his right forearm while making a forward leap to the left. With your right hand, the back of it uppermost, grab his right arm above the elbow and pull it to you (fig. 18, above). With your left hand push his forearm behind his body and hoist his elbow upward, sliding your hand so that it comes to rest on his right shoulder blade (fig. 19). Keep your body weight on the elbow to keep it bent. Place the interior edge of your forearm on his adam's apple, with your right hand gripping his left shoulder or his uniform. Lift your left elbow while pulling the enemy to the ground with your right arm (fig 20).

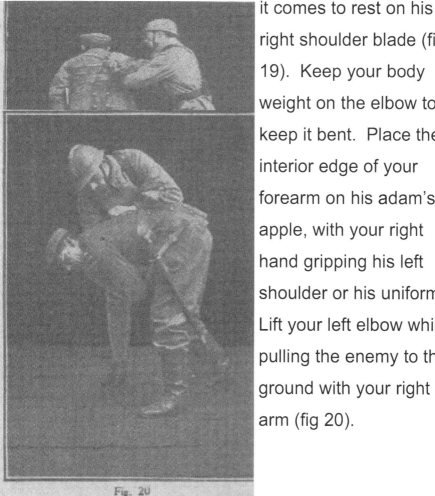

Fig. 20

II. Regarding bayonet

attacks

Throw an object of some kind into the enemy's face (if you have nothing else, throw your helmet) and jump to one side, pushing the weapon away from you (fig. 21). Jump on the foe and strangle or trip him to strip him of his weapon and stab him (fig. 22 & 23).

NOTE: No matter what the object, a stick, or even a short object like a bayonet in your hand or a knife will make it easier to turn aside the enemy's thrust.

If after the block you have managed to seize the enemy's weapon, grab it with both hands and twist it to make the enemy let go, then turn the weapon on him. If he resists try a chassé kick or a knee strike to his genitals to aid in stripping the weapon.

Fig. 23

Fig 22

(A Practical Guide to training for Army recruits. September 1st, 1917).

CHAPTER IV

TAKING A PRISONER

"Let's go!"

With your right hand grab his right wrist, the palm of his hand turned upward. Put yourself right up against him by pivoting. Lift your left arm and pass it around his right arm with your forearm placed above his elbow, your hand coming to rest on your own right forearm or your belt buckle. Now lead him away (fig. 24). If the prisoner resists, roughly increase the pressure with your left arm and bring your right hand down while turning his wrist outward. This hold is also used from the other side.

Fig. 24

Printed in Great Britain
by Amazon